ALSO BY JANE COOPER

The Weather of Six Mornings

Maps & Windows

MAPS & WINDOWS

POEMS

JANE COOPER

COLLIER BOOKS
A Division of Macmillan Publishing Co., Inc.
NEW YORK

COLLIER MACMILLAN PUBLISHERS
LONDON

ACKNOWLEDGMENTS

Some of the poems in Part I first appeared in *The American Poetry Review*, *The Nation*, *Sarah Lawrence Journal*, *The Transatlantic Review*, *Voyages* and in *Essays from Sarah Lawrence Faculty* for February, 1974. "The Weather of Six Mornings," "Feathers" (under the title "March") and "No More Elegies" were first published in slightly different form by *The New Yorker*. The Cabral translation was sponsored by The Academy of American Poets, appeared in *The Hudson Review* and was included, also in slightly different form, in *An Anthology of Twentieth-Century Brazilian Poetry* (Wesleyan University Press), edited by Elizabeth Bishop and Emanuel Brasil. Of the poems in Part III, "Obligations," in a later version, was originally printed in *New Poets of England and America, Second Selection* (Meridian), edited by Donald Hall and Robert Pack, and others appeared recently in *The American Poetry Review* and *No More Masks: An Anthology of Poems by Women* (Doubleday), edited by Florence Howe and Ellen Bass. *The American Poetry Review* first published the prose of Part II.

Macmillan Publishing Co., Inc.
866 Third Avenue, New York, N. Y. 10022
Collier-Macmillan Canada Ltd.

Library of Congress Cataloging in Publication Data

Cooper, Jane, 1924–
    Maps & windows.

    Includes bibliographical references.
    1. Cooper, Jane, 1924–   I. Title.
PS3553.059M3   811'.5'4   74–10975
ISBN 0–02–069300–1 (pbk.)

FIRST COLLIER BOOKS EDITION 1974

Maps & Windows is also published in a hardcover edition by Macmillan Publishing Co., Inc.

Printed in the United States of America

For my sister Rachel

I am grateful to the Ingram Merrill Foundation for a grant during 1971–72 that provided the freedom for new poems. I am also grateful to Yaddo and The MacDowell Colony, where much work was actually done and where I had time for some of the thinking about poetry that has been important to me. My special thanks to my brother and the friends whose sympathy made the form of this book imaginable and whose criticisms helped me to shape and reshape Part II—in particular Betty Kray, Grace Paley, Adrienne Rich, Muriel Rukeyser, and Jean Valentine.

Contents

Maps & Windows

I

Calling Me from Sleep

New & Selected Poems

1961–1973

My Young Mother

My young mother, her face narrow
and dark with unresolved wishes
under a hatbrim of the twenties,
stood by my middleaged bed.

Still as a child pretending sleep
to a grownup watchful or calling,
I lay in a corner of my dream
staring at the mole above her lip.

Familiar mole! but that girlish look
as if I had nothing to give her—
Eyes blue—brim dark—
calling me from sleep after decades.

1964

In the House of the Dying

So once again, hearing the tired aunts
whisper together under the kitchen globe,
I turn away; I am not one of them.

At the sink I watch the water cover my hands
in a sheath of light. Upstairs she lies alone
dreaming of autumn nights when her children were born.

On the steps between us grows in a hush of waiting
the impossible silence between two generations.
The aunts buzz on like flies around a bulb.

I am dressed like them. Standing with my back turned
I wash the dishes in the same easy way.
Only at birth and death do I utterly fail.

For death is my old friend who waits on the stairs.
Whenever I pass I nod to him like the newsman
who is there every day; for them he is the priest.

While the birth of love is so terrible to me
I feel unworthy of the commonest marriage.
Upstairs she lies, washed through by the two miracles.

1961

Letters

1

That quiet point of light
trembled and went out.

Iron touches a log:
it crumbles to coal, then ashes.

The log sleeps in its shape.
A new moon rises.

Darling my white body
still bears your imprint.

2

Wind chewed the screen,
rain clawed my window.

Outside three crows
make their harsh rainy scraping.

Autumn has come
in early July.

On the ground white petals:
my rain-soaked letters.

1965

The Weather of Six Mornings

1

Sunlight lies along my table
like abandoned pages.

I try to speak
of what is so hard for me

—this clutter of a life—
Puritanical signature!

In the prolonged heat insects,
pine needles, birch leaves

make a ground bass of silence
that never quite dies.

Treetops are shuddering
in uneasy clusters

like rocking water
whirlpooled before a storm.

Words knock at my breast,
heave and struggle to get out.

A black-capped bird
pecks on, unafraid.

Yield then, yield
to the invading rustle of the rain!

All is closed in
by an air so rain-drenched

the distant barking of tied-up dogs
ripples to the heart of the woods.

Only a man's voice
refuses to be absorbed.

Hearing of your death
by a distant roadside

I wanted to erect some marker
though your ashes float out to sea.

4

If the weather breaks
I can speak of your dying,

if the weather breaks,
if the crows stop calling

and flying low
(again today there is thunder, out-

lying . . .)
I can speak of your living,

the lightning-flash of meeting,
the green leaves waving at our windows.

Yesterday a letter
spoke of our parting—

a kind of dissolution
so unlike this sudden stoppage.

Now all the years in between
flutter away like lost poems.

And the morning light is so delicate,
so utterly empty. . . .

at high altitude, after long illness,
breathing in mote by mote a vanished world. . . .

Rest.
A violin bow, a breeze

just touches the birches.
Cheep—a new flute

tunes up in a birch top.
A chipmunk's warning skirrs. . . .

Whose foot disturbs these twigs?
To the sea of received silence

why should I sign
my name?

1965

Feathers

I've died, but you are still living!
The pines are still living, and the eastern sky.
Today a great bustle rocks the treetops
of snow and sunshine, dry branches, green brooms.

The pines are cleaning their attics.
Mercilessly, they snap off weak twigs.
If I look down from my window
I can see one of the walks we used to take together.

The snow is covered with brown feathers.
In the fields it's as if an army had just limped by,
leaving its slight corpses, abandoned weapons—
a wreckage that will melt into spring.

Nearby is a little grove; on brown needles
we lay side by side telling each other stories.
Against the glass here, listen—
Nothing can stop the huzzah of the male wind!

1967

Hunger Moon

The last full moon of February
stalks the fields; barbed wire casts a shadow.
Rising slowly, a beam moved toward the west
stealthily changing position

until now, in the small hours, across the snow
it advances on my pillow
to wake me, not rudely like the sun
but with the cocked gun of silence.

I am alone in a vast room
where a vain woman once slept.
The moon, in pale buckskins, crouches
on guard beside her bed.

Slowly the light wanes, the snow will melt
and all the fences thrum in the spring breeze
but not until that sleeper, trapped
in my body, turns and turns.

1967

El Sueño de la Razón

(for a young poet in a mental hospital)

Cousin, it's of you I always dream
as I walk these dislocated lawns
or compose a stanza under the Corot trees.

The music of my walking reconciles
somewhat the clipped but common ground
with the lost treetops' thunderous heads.

How they are always muttering in the still
afternoon; how they create
their own darkness under hottest sun.

They compose clouds or a sea
so far above us we can scarcely tell
why such a premonition brushes our cheeks.

Yet as I walk I scan
the woods for a girl's white figure
slipping away among the pines' thin shafts.

Hiding, she is hiding, and in your dreams
the poem's cleared spaces
barely hold out against the stately riot

of marching trees, a suddenly Turner sky.
Poor furious girl, our voices sound
alike, your nurse told me, discreet and gentle.

1967

No More Elegies

Everyone rushed into town
right after coffee, though the icy ruts
are gray as iron, and icicles
two feet long scarcely drip.

The sun is so bright on the snow
I'm out tramping in dark beach glasses.
A clump of leafless birches
steams against a dark blue sky.

Over there the yellow frame
of some new construction glints,
while the tips of those bushes are bloody
as if tomorrow, tomorrow would be Easter!

And a phoebe is calling, calling,
all the small birds come fluting from the pines:
No more elegies! No more elegies! Poor
fools, it's not even spring!

1967

In Silence Where We Breathe

As a boy he was so silent
she raged like a gnat. Summer nights—

Summer nights he stood at his desk
wrapped in a wordless soprano.

Once he constructed a clipper ship
to scale from the *Century Dictionary*.

All May they ran barefoot
through the stinging southern streets.

The air was like mercury,
a heavy silver ball.

And the river stank of salt
and rotten magnolia candles

down the end of the block—Slot machines!
From their grandmother's veranda

she could hear the ring of life
start out through a swing door—

No one could tell such stories;
but he never cried, not once.

1967

Poetry As Continuity

The young doctor dreamed of revolution.
The middleaged revolutionary dreamed of a tree
offering its red berries, thrusting down roots like a woman.

Under miles of snow, under railroad tracks stitched like a
    suture,
the earth slept all the way to Moscow.
How strangely space is playing the part of time!

What reached the city was only a coincidence
in a life of parades. Zhivago,
you are all we have left, in the end you were scarcely a man.

1970

Cemetery in Pernambuco:
Our Lady of Light

(*from the* Portuguese *of João Cabral de Melo Neto*)

Nobody lies in this earth
because no river is at rest
in any other river, nor is the sea
a potter's field of rivers.

None of these dead men here
comes dressed in a coffin.
Therefore they are not buried
but spilled out on the ground.

Wrapped in the hammocks they slept in,
naked to sun and rain,
they come bringing their own flies.
The ground fits them like a glove.

Dead, they lived in the open air.
Today they are part of open earth,
so much the earth's that the earth
does not feel their intrusion.

1970

Things

Things have their own lives here. The hall chairs
count me as I climb the steps. The piano
is playing at will from behind three potted plants,
while the photograph of the dead girl in the luminescent hat
glows pink since the lamp lighted itself at four.

We are very humane here. Of course people
go off course sometimes, radio to the outside world
only through typewriter noise or the bathwater running.
And then the empty glasses, the books on health food left
   around. . . .
But the things have been here longer than we have.

And the trees are older even than furniture.
They were here to witness the original drownings
(because I always think the children drowned, no matter
   what you say).
Last night a voice called me from outside my door.
It was no one's voice, perhaps it came from the umbrella
   stand.

1971

Souvenirs

Anyway we are always waking
in bedrooms of the dead, smelling
musk of their winter jackets, tracking
prints of their heels across our blurred carpets.

So why hang onto a particular postcard?
If a child's lock of hair brings back
the look of that child, shall I
nevertheless not let it blow away?

Houses, houses, we lodge in such husks!
inhabit such promises, seeking the unborn
in a worn-out photograph, hoping to break free
even of our violent and faithful lives.

1970–71

Inheritances

Malte Laurids, peevish: *And one has*
nothing and nobody, travels about the world
with a few clothes and a satchel of books. What sort of life
is it? without a house, without
inheritances (the Chamberlain's eyeglasses, say,
in a glass case?), *without*
dogs—

Yet he wrote the Chamberlain's death, explaining:
I have taken action against fear, I
have sat all night and written.

And: *Still it is not enough*
to have memories, they
must turn to blood inside you.

1971

A Circle, a Square, a Triangle and a Ripple of Water

Sex floated like a moon
over the composition. Home
was transpierced, ego
thrust out of line and
shaded. But sex floated
over the unconscious, pulling it
up like a sea in points to
where she dreamed, rolling
on and on, immaculate, a full moon
or a breast full of milk.
Seemingly untouched she
was the stone at the center of
the pool whose circles
shuddered off around her.

1971

Suicide Note

It's not that I'm out of touch—
a child stranded on a shoal
looking back without feeling
at the grownups still playing on the beach.

It's just that everyone else's
needs seem so urgent!
Already I've ceased to exist
at my end of this conversation—

And I wanted to defend you!
The telephone is the invader.
Wreath of electrodes! Love!
No trespassing beyond this point. Anyone found here
   with dog or gun will be

1971

A Nightmare of the Suburbs

I'll be in my own room, upstairs,
the door locked, with a gun—
But nobody's coming
yet,

no black bodies
rising like night-flowers from your leafy summer streets,
no axe that splits
the drowsy thighbones of your window frame.

You look in your hand mirror—
They won't get in without a struggle!

But already the meager body
of the pistol begins to wake from his long sleep
of cardboard in the drawer of your bedside table.

Glowing blue-black,
now that he's here
only blood can appease him.

1971

The Earthquake

Two people wakened suddenly by an earthquake
accuse each other: *You pushed me out of bed!*
The floor is cold, they're disgruntled, they start to laugh.
Back to bed. The little hills
just beginning to show dark along the horizon
fold their paws and shove off to sleep again
embracing privacy.

But what can I say for the one who sleeps alone
in a child's cot? *Another dream?*
She imagines she must have parachuted out of bed
to escape.
She accuses herself.
Stubbornly, in a mummy-roll of blankets,
she lies awake explaining her usual day.

1973

Pencil Sketch of Self & Other

When you kissed me it was as if
someone had just stepped lightly out of the room.

How shy I was in any crowd,
and you, how adept!

How I kept you waiting
longer than any boy uncertain of his sex!

Your mother, musical, suicidal,
slept with a thread tied round her nurse's finger

(so I learned a few details); your father
photographed beside his swimming pool. . . .

How we almost ruined each other, you
with your hope of children,

I with my body which I took too seriously,
that stunned room. . . .

A story, like *The Garden Party*,
no longer even possible.

Yet I want to forgive us both
as if it still matters.

1972–73

Waiting

My body knows it will never bear children.
What can I say to my body now,
this used violin?
Every night it cries out desolately
from its secret cave.

Old body, old friend,
why are you so unforgiving?

Why are you so stiff and resistant
clenched around empty space?
An instrument is not a box.

But suppose you are an empty box?
Suppose you are like that famous wooden music hall in Troy,
    New York,
waiting to be torn down
where the orchestras love to play?

Let compassion breathe in and out of you
filling you with poems.

1971

Nothing Has Been Used in the Manufacture of This Poetry That Could Have Been Used in the Manufacture of Bread

A LONG TIME AGO I had a student who was married to a tug-boat captain. She had three babies and used to get up at five in the morning to write her stories before the children woke. The reasons why she was finding it hard to do the writing that was in her were not far to seek, yet she and her husband, who were Catholic, expected a still larger family. I have no idea what happened to that young woman; perhaps she is back at her typewriter now, with the last child in school. But more than two decades of teaching women, talented, intellectually curious and passionately eager to live their lives, have convinced me she's not an isolated example. Tillie Olsen, in particular, has written movingly of the "Silences When Writers Don't Write," of women's silences, and at the same time of her own desire to cry out at H. H. Richardson, the Australian novelist ("There are enough women to do the childbearing and childrearing. I know of none who can write my books."): "Yes, and I know of none who can bear and rear my children either!"

Women, we imagine, have always written, since when-ever they learned their letters—just as in preliterate times they must have been storytellers and weavers of legends alongside men. This being the case, why have so many stopped? Or, if they kept on, why have so few pub-lished? Such questions are very much in the air right now, and the commonest answer—following Olsen—is that marriage along the old, accepted lines and, especially, child-bearing and childrearing can sap energy, privacy, a sense of the earned right to write. The last invasion may well be the most serious one. "Them lady poets must not marry, pal," declares John Berryman's Henry in one of the Dream Songs, suggesting also—oh, but don't we all recognize what he suggests?

I've never married, have no children, so you could say my case was always different. Yet from the age of twenty-two to the age of twenty-six, I worked strenuously and perfectly seriously on a book of poems (a *book*, not just poems), then "gave up poetry" and never tried to publish but one of them. Why? Does this mean the same injunctions have affected all women, not just the wives and mothers? Haven't we been most deeply shaped in our very expectations of ourselves, and isn't this what has been most daunting? In fact, since I was unmarried and belonged to a marrying generation, was I in a special way vulnerable to the unspoken words: "What sort of woman are you?"

While I was working on my book, I told people I didn't believe in magazine publication because all my poems were related. Privately, I felt the poems were never finished. I suspect most privately of all, I couldn't face living out the full range of intuition they revealed. Later, after I'd come back to writing and was beginning to publish in magazines and anthologies, the old poems still seemed to throw off balance whatever I was currently doing. After 1956 or so, I only remember looking at them once until comparatively recently. For a while I told myself I'd destroyed them. They turned up on a lower shelf of my bookcase, in an old Christmas-card box, along with drafts and drafts of later and often less striking work.

Two winters ago friends looking at some new manuscripts of mine announced I was changing. The new poems seemed more tense, more aggressive than those in my first printed book, *The Weather of Six Mornings*, written mostly during my thirties and finally published in 1969. And it's true that book is full of acceptances, apparently traditional but hard won. Above all the self is seen as no more important than anyone else, a self in a world of selves who give one another strength and life. (One poem, for my mother, ends "How can I tell which one of us is absent?" The book ends "why should I sign / my name?") I said no, I thought I was just getting back to something closer to the mood of my earliest work. Earliest work? I hesitated, made excuses, but before long the living-room floor was carpeted with dozens of old yellow scratch sheets.

Now I was the one to be surprised. For one thing, there were many more poems than I'd imagined: eighty-odd in all. Then, there were some good, complete poems I had no recollection of writing. It was a shock to discover that at some point, probably in the mid-fifties, I'd thought enough of the poems to go through and date a number of them; also that where various drafts existed, I'd as often as not made a poem less rather than more interesting. Some poems got angrier and sharper and less abstract as they went along, but others lost their initial honesty and became over-complicated. This was particularly true of poems which I'd tried to rewrite between 1952 and 1954, after the impulse toward that first collection was spent. Finally, it was a shock to find that I'd forgotten, or distorted, or perhaps never truly faced what the book was "about."

What I Had Told Myself

What I had told myself, what I remember telling myself in my twenties, was that I was writing a book of war poems from a civilian's, a woman's, point of view. World War II was the war I grew up into. I was fourteen when England and France declared war on Germany (and I came from a fiercely internationally-minded, interventionist family, except that my brother, just older than myself, was for a short time a pacifist); I was seventeen at the time of Pearl Harbor; the first atomic bombs were dropped on Hiroshima and Nagasaki, and peace treaties were signed, just before my senior year in college. From 1946 to 1950, my most intense writing years, I lived in Princeton, which was full of returned veterans studying on the G.I. Bill. I was even an associate member of a veterans' group which met to discuss issues like the implementation of the Marshall Plan. In the summer of 1947 I went to England and France before it was possible to do so unless you had a reason recognized by a foreign government. I went to study at the first Oxford Summer School, along with many students and professors from the great pre-war universities of Europe; these men and women, wearing heavy sandals and with worn, stained shirt collars, I found in a state of euphoria because they could talk to one another for the first time in eight years. London was still full of bombed-out sites that were being converted into "car parks," except there were few cars. Wherever I walked a single hammer could be heard tapping. In late August I crossed the Channel. At Boulogne the only solid things left in the landscape were the German fortifications and submarine pens, with here and there a foundered Allied invasion ship. Elsewhere along the French coast the V-2 rocket pens still humped up like molehills made of cement. In Paris I saw a sign in a department-store window that read, over a display of wicker furniture: NOTHING HAS BEEN USED IN THE MANUFACTURE OF THIS FURNITURE THAT COULD HAVE BEEN USED IN THE MANUFACTURE OF BREAD.

How everything looked, what the European professors said, changed my life, quite simply. I find I wrote home in the middle of that summer: "I woke the other morning with the realization that I should have to write, and probably write poetry. This made me feel foolish, more than anything else. I distrust poets, and have been fighting the idea for about five years now. Just as I have been fighting the idea of teaching. But perhaps they are both necessary."

At Oxford our tutors were members of the Oxford Extra-Mural Delegacy, which during the winters sent men and women into rural villages to conduct workers' education courses in literature, history, social philosophy, that were to run for four consecutive years. This project had the blessing of the post-Churchill Labor Government. It was a kind of teaching I had never really imagined, despite having graduated from a State University which had a whole campus dedicated to agronomy, for the sake of its constituent farmers, and ran "short courses" in cheese-making. At Oxford also our tutors read poetry aloud to us in the evenings, something that rarely happened in those days in the United States; readings, like chamber music, had been popular in the bomb shelters, the Underground stations, during the London blitz. The European professors never tired of quoting poems to one another in Czech, Russian or Polish, French. For the first time poetry presented itself to me as a means of survival.

So I went home in September not to start to write (for I had written poems all during high school and had recently begun again after a long wartime silence) but with a focus. This war had been, I thought, peculiarly a civilians' war, the war of the bombed-out cities and of ruined, isolated country houses in northern France. Even now, two years later, the dark bread, made of potatoes or sometimes even sawdust, flattened almost to the tabletop when you pressed it with a sharp knife. . . . I thought, at the same time, that all wars are probably total for the people living through them; the Hundred Years' War must have been a total civilians' war. For civilians, read women—women-and-children, women-and-the-sick-and-the-old. Yet of course, women had not just been civilians during World War II, not just the passive receivers of suffering. At Oxford I knew a young Frenchwoman who had been a member of the Resistance; my best English friend was just out of the WRENS, the women's branch of the Royal Navy. I had myself spent several terms at college studying to be a meteorologist—astronomy, navigation, physics—with the difference that I hadn't really needed to, in America where women were never drafted, and after a while I had switched to languages, with some vague idea (since I imagined the war would go on and on) of a translating job with the O.S.S.

I would write as a noncombatant, a witness. It was the air war I was most haunted by, since my brother, my father, my uncle, my brother-in-law had all been involved in aviation in some form during the war years. I never could get over the peculiar beauty of a bombed-out landscape (which needless to say I only saw once the worst had been cleaned up, once the summer field flowers—poppies and fireweed and ragwort—had seeded themselves and started blooming over the rubble); nor my guilt because I found the desolation visually beautiful. I had two friends from childhood, now returned veterans, who had been shot down as pilots over Europe and imprisoned; one later made his way to Ravensbruck and helped with survivors of the concentration camp there. I hated the very idea of war, all its details, yet obviously, I was excited and absorbed by it, and also I felt guilty because I had not participated in any direct way, only through association. And how could you write except from experience?

Perhaps, as Grace Paley has suggested, this was one of the true problems of women writers at that time. The men's lives seemed more central than ours, almost more truthful. They had been shot down, or squirmed up the beaches. We had waited for their letters. Again, I was not a European or an Englishwoman. Yet when I hesitated to comment on Dylan Thomas's "A Refusal to Mourn the Death, by Fire, of a Child in London," then quite a new poem, in my Oxford seminar, because I had not lived through the blitz, my tutor said soberly, "Thank God you were spared that."

And even now I have to ask myself: Why did I feel the need to write about the holocaust almost more than individual human relations, or, to disguise my purpose to myself? What fascination with the will, as well as sympathy, did that reflect?

Hearing poems read aloud in the long, light Oxford evenings brought not only Thomas but, even more vividly, Hopkins and Yeats alive for me. Was it for this reason, I wonder, that all the poets I turned to when I started to write again were neither Americans nor women? What would have happened if I'd listened to William Carlos Williams instead, with his love for casual American speech rhythms, or if I'd valued Emily Dickinson more? Auden was out of favor in England when I was there, because after serving as a model of political engagement during the thirties, he had come to the United States just before the outbreak of World War II, thus escaping much of what he had helped others prepare their minds for. A copout, it seemed to the young tutors, who stubbornly read us Day Lewis and Mac-Neice instead. But I'd long been familiar with the work of Auden and also Spender, and when I thought of a contemporary, politically aware tone of voice, that was the tone I still thought in. Because of my work in languages, I was also steeped in the poetry of García Lorca, with its mixture of surrealism and peoples' theater, but it was only much later that I could begin to understand what that combination might mean to me.

"A Book of War Poems"

Had I published my book of poems in 1950 or '51 or '52, as I suppose could have happened, it would certainly not have been the same collection I now call *Mercator's World*. It would have been longer, rougher and more mixed in tone, and it would have contained many more political poems. It would have been more like (though still not clearly) "a book of war poems from a woman's point of view." For especially to begin with, war and its survivors made up much of my conscious subject matter; and even my imagery (which is not, as Adrienne Rich has pointed out, a product of our conscious choice so much as it is something thrown up on our consciousness, like our dreams) was dominated by explosions, mapmaking and stars and navigation, and scientific discovery. I was writing with a curious amalgam of seventeenth-century and twentieth-century references. Behind the American atomic-bomb tests in the Pacific in 1946, I perceived the *hubris* of Kepler (nevertheless a genuinely religious man), and the fact that the first silk I saw after five years of wartime was a parachutist's landing chart, made into a woman's headscarf, somehow got mixed up in my mind with my father's collection of early European maps of the discovery and colonization of Florida. Most of these maps were based on Mercator's projection, with its squared-off yet strangely exaggerated perspectives. If "Mercator's world" was in an obvious sense my father's world, it also suggested a habit of thinking that, distorted and then followed down to its logical end (as Einstein's theory prepared the way for the hydrogen bomb, which Einstein protested), had plunged us into global conflict for the second time in a generation.

Not that my imagery was only a kind of large abstract grid taken from warmaking and the physics of fission and light. There are also specific human images in many of the early poems that still have the power to take me a bit by surprise and so to move me.

> In bomb shelters many are honest
> As Jews are
> Pierced by the knowledge of bullets in bullet-proof cars.

was written even before I went abroad. Until I reread a line about German children holding out their palms to beg as a closed train blurs by, I'd forgotten that civilian trains were still sealed in the Occupied Zones in 1947. And a P.O.W. coming back to New York

> like a man off an operating table,
> A tangible silence around him, an ether cone,
> While American tastes and words in his mouth glitter
> Like knocked-out teeth

is dazed by his own inarticulateness: "his bell of glass / Which keeps even the girls he kisses from touching his face."

Perhaps it is important that these poems were begun in a climate which, while it countenanced—with a good deal of furor—the Bikini bomb tests, saw the making of the United Nations, the Marshall Plan and other schemes for the reconstruction of Europe, and not long afterward the first Fulbright scholarships. And although the reasons were certainly more personal than political, I wonder if it is wholly irrelevant that the poems ended, trickled away, at about the point when the McCarthy hearings became possible?

Now that we turn against the whole notion that the United States should be a moral leader in world affairs—as if we could tell others what to feel and how to govern themselves—it's hard to remember the optimism and seriousness of the first couple of years after the end of World War II, when many people, including many returned veterans, felt responsible for rebuilding Europe and Japan physically and economically and, above all, for restoring communications among nations. I think some of that optimism got into my poems, at least in the form of a confidence that I could write them. Several are positive statements of international responsibility. At the same time, there is some hopelessness that we (that is, Americans), or at least I myself, could ever rise above the fact that our experiences had *not* been those of the damaged civilian populations:

> For past a certain knowledge
> Of headlines there can be no sharing. . . .
>
> And Europe's children cease to live
> For a moment in our minds
> And a certain bombed corner kind-
> ly obliterates itself. . . .

It was a celebration of spring, that poem!

Another poem asks what happens to peasants in a war ("Women go / On sweeping out the house where they were killed"), while exploring the state of mind of the wisest human beings, which I saw as a kind of recovered innocence, knowledge tempered by extremes of mental and physical suffering. I couldn't forget the two Czech professors in my Oxford seminar who, even in 1947, no longer looked forward to political freedom but used to argue endlessly over how, under totalitarian conditions, one could preserve free-

dom of the spirit. I concluded that "Universal concern is
not enough." "The great gas chambers of the mind shut
down" on whatever we fail to accomplish in our own per-
sons. Struggling to define my own religious consciousness
between the poles of Christianity and Existentialism, I
prayed, "Why, while cities burn, do I still live?"

> I have no faith. I do not expect to recover
> Any but myself, the unit, man.
> Mass charity affects me like an ether
> Empty of consciousness as of its pain.

The Archipelago of Love

"Not enough scherzi," said my brother affectionately,
when my 1969 book came out, and indeed I consider it a
great weakness in my writing that I'm so shy about dealing
with joy. For I've known real joys in my life, and the
period I'm talking about was unusually full of them. The
war, though it obsessed me, was over. Horizons were ex-
panding not only geographically and politically but per-
sonally for me. The men were back. I was living in a men's
university town. When I think of the year 1948, I can
hardly remember times when I was alone (though there
must have been some, while I worked on my poems or
finished another half-day's stint of freelance editing). What
I remember instead is tramping across fields or driving in an
open car with one companion or another; climbing the scaf-
folding of some new postwar housing because I was excited
about architecture; sitting in on seminars on literature or
philosophy and then talking afterward under a dogwood
tree or hunched over bowls of homemade soup at a student
restaurant. Or, later, when it seemed as if some kind of
decision must be drawing near, there were the evenings of
mutual silence and intense, diffident questionings.

Marriage was on everybody's mind in those days, men's
as well as women's, after the fragmentation of the war, and
most of my friends wanted three or four babies as soon as

they could afford them. For the veterans studying on the G.I. Bill, there was a rush to put down roots, to "get started." Still, it was curiously difficult, if you hadn't married during the war, to imagine how a peacetime relationship could develop slowly and quietly and reach fruition without the drastic backdrop of wartime leaves, wartime ultimatums. I sometimes wonder if I knew how to make a decision for several years after I stopped reading casualty lists. On the windowsills of the dormitories were large metal stars giving the names of former Princeton students who had occupied rooms there and been killed; often they were names I knew. Yet I used to feel a kind of outrageous triumph, an elation that seemed as if it would grow and grow and might take over everything. I was young, alive, free, learning to know myself and others, learning my craft of poetry, all my senses were opening.

So, no matter what headlines I gave my work, from the first I was exploring other territory: "Look where the archipelago of love / Lies at our feet, the waves washing like fever, / Conscious, unconscious. . . ." The earliest complete poem in this volume, "Eve," written when I was just twenty-three, is a poem of sexual awakening, frankly acknowledged. "In the spume / Of a triple wave she lives: sperm, / Man and life's mate break like flags upon her shore." What can I say now to those images of conquest? At the same time the sexual over-view ("Marriage must take her now, or . . .") shows how much I was still living within a social pattern, or at least a pattern of expectation, as clearly defined as the physical world had once seemed to be according to Mercator's projection. Out of the tension between that enclosing, conservative order and my own expanding vision and senses grew what I have come to recognize as the strongest and most valid part of my early work.

For here, as was not true of the war poems, there could be no question of authenticity. Despite the limitations on sexual roles which the poems alternately question and confirm, relationships between women and men were seen in

41 | *The Manufacture of Poetry*

individual terms and, increasingly, with unsparing eyes. It was in 1948 that I wrote "The Door" (other versions speak of "this double door"), which is a plea for equality and for not being treated as a sexual object. While this poem seems simply honest today, I wonder how it would have sounded had it been published at the time? Interestingly, I wasn't really able to face all it said myself. The draft I finally settled on is not the one printed on page 64 but one which cut out the lines "I am / A person after all, you are / A person . . ." and substituted at the end a vision of almost supernatural union. Having asked the man not to be a god, did I get scared? Somehow I was trying, in imagination, to revive some perfect model of the trap I had to spring.

Perhaps not surprisingly, many of the poems that were inherently most full of love and growth were distanced by their forms. This too was part of the world, social and literary, that surrounded me. Probably it was also part of my own mind-set. "Eve" is modeled on sonnets by Hopkins. I wrote a lot of songs, following seventeenth-century examples as well as Yeats and Auden. These stay with me now mainly for what they reveal in spite of, not because of, their manners. "I guard my independence / Which beautifully guards / Me . . ." seems chilling in its implications. More sympathetic is a song written for a friend on his thirtieth birthday, though again, I can't help speculating on what it might have meant to other women had it come out when it was composed:

> *En l'an trentiesme de mon aage*
> Perhaps I shall be wiser,
> More certain than I am here
> In the coils of my heritage.
>
> *Que toutes mes hontes j'eus bues—*
> At twenty-three
> I am caught in such necessity
> To be a man, the crowd's hero,

> *Que toutes mes hontes j'eus bues.*
> I would be double,
> Half lover-poet-sybil,
> Half what the kind nets swallow. . . .

Did I want to be a man? Not that I can remember, certainly not sexually. But I must have thought that "To be a man, the crowd's hero" was what becoming a published poet would mean; it was where my ambition was driving me. Then the definition changes to something female but disturbing: "Half lover-poet-sybil." How could you be a sybil by halves? I recognized, though I still did not fully recognize, the doubleness of my urge to become. What was expected of me, what I wanted for myself in the most profound ways, was marriage and children. I saw the "nets" as "kind," even though they were also the "coils" of my middle-class heritage. (And I was still living at home.) I didn't really think you could be double. At Iowa, some years later, a classmate told me he believed that to be a woman poet was "a contradiction in terms." But by then I had gone back to writing, and for keeps.

> john berryman asked me to write a poem about roosters.
> elizabeth bishop, he said, once wrote a poem about roosters.
> *do your poems use capital letters?* he asked. *like god?*
> i said. *god no,* he said, *like princeton!*

There is something in this rhyme that even today brings back the rollicking fall afternoon when Berryman, then a young instructor and no more than a campus acquaintance, rushed across the college lawn and without even pausing to say hello began to tell me how to write my poems! Not because of what it says (I recorded the conversation verbatim and virtually in its entirety) but because it catches some of the laughter yet also bewilderment I felt at "the company of poets," where "the masculine thing to do," etc.

Princeton truly was a male stronghold in those days, and

no doubt this intensified my own sense of a dichotomy between "woman" and "poet." I knew a number of men who wrote but no women. Work by women was still only sparsely represented in contemporary poetry anthologies. Now that I have a number of women friends who are poets, it's hard to recall the particular kind of isolation I felt in my writing or my almost beleaguered self-questioning.

I do remember how, when I was about fourteen, my sister had brought home from Vassar Muriel Rukeyser's first two books and I had a sudden glimpse of a young woman, not much older than my sister, who was out in the world writing poems; it seemed a life of extraordinary courage. I continued to hear about Rukeyser from time to time. Otherwise, men's praise of women's poetry didn't seem to go much beyond Marianne Moore and Elizabeth Bishop, whose work I admired but couldn't then *use*, in the deep sense that writers use the discoveries of other writers as steps toward their own growth. Somehow I had absorbed out of the New Critical air itself (because I honestly don't remember anyone's telling me so) that women have trouble managing traditional meters with authority and verve and also can't handle long lines. Emily Dickinson's lines were short, and besides, since I knew only the bowdlerized, smoothed-over versions of her poems, it didn't occur to me how original she could be musically within those repeated New England hymn tunes. So I went to school to what models I could find—mostly the British poets already mentioned—to learn long rhythmic periods and metrical invention within the forms. The subjects I was writing about—war and relations between women and men—seemed also mostly to have remained the property of men.

I'm afraid it is typical—the year was still only 1948—that I was at my most "literary" when I wrote a loose theme-and-variations using characters from *The Tempest* as voices for my own deep-seated fears:

Prospero:
> Health is what I have to buy for my children.
> If I ransom grace, that dream of prows and discovery
> And all except a physical creation,
> Do you think I can have it? will the stirrings of the air
>   let me?

Miranda:
> O sweet Ariel, sweet strings who play with the idea of pain
> Not feeling it, who don't take in the cost
> Of following music suffered by the brain
> And not the blood, can't you hear the sailors cry *All's lost!*

That first line was, I know, meant quite literally. I was concerned for my unborn children if I persisted in being a writer, not primarily devoted to "a physical creation." Never very strong, I questioned whether I would have the energy to be a good mother unless I gave up other options.

The second stanza is still more complicated. For the old worry that to write might mean to wait on the sidelines, not really to act and suffer and "exist," which was present in the poems about wartime as guilt at nonparticipation, was now beginning to be metamorphosed into a conflict between writing and my own sexuality. Here, as Miranda follows "music suffered by the brain / And not the blood," it is the "sailors" who cry *All's lost!* In a very early poem I had written "Everyone's childhood lies buried in the sea." Several years later, in the poem "Meteors," I was to make the farseeing, less physical (as I thought then) artist–lover into the "aviator," who suffers only in imagination as he bombs, while the "sailor," the lover who promises sexual and family satisfaction, lies mired in his very physicality. Almost half *Mercator's World*, and in particular the poems of 1949 and 1950, explore, on the one hand, the dilemma of a woman artist in love with a man who is not an artist and who therefore can't altogether share her cravings ("Could you construct a me / All physical reality?") and, on the other hand, the dilemma of one in love with a fellow artist ("I still remember evenings when I learned / The tricks of style . . ."). In a poem finished just before I stopped writing, "In a Room with Picassos," the woman artist is questioning not only the male artist but the tools of her own art, that is, the morality of her creative impulse.

Even that 1947 poem about "the archipelago of love," written out of all my dazzled awareness of the possibilities ahead of me and called "Design for an Odyssey," ends

> But perhaps our gods are weak, those islands useless
>
> Where they lie bright-eyed on the field of our illusion,
> White and flat like a fleet of summer boats.
> Suppose they are really too small and we sail alone
> Past the antipodes of desire and doubt?

Questions of Autobiography

But poetry isn't autobiography, and if some of the poems I've quoted from here most extensively were more successful, I probably wouldn't use them in the same way. For what poetry must do is alert us to a truth, and it must be necessary; once it exists, we realize how much we needed exactly this. Writing about the war was important for me personally, but I didn't, couldn't have much to say about it that could be fresh for others—as, for instance, Dylan Thomas's "A Refusal to Mourn" and "Holy Spring" had brought me up short when I first read them in the little book *Deaths and Entrances*, standing in a London bookstall, wondering if I could afford to buy. In the end, my book was never "a book of war poems from a woman's point of view," for the reason that the real discoveries I was making in those days were being documented in the poems about man–woman relationships, which nevertheless depended on a lot of the same imagery. The most truthful poem I was to write about World War II—the elegy called "The Faithful"—didn't come along until 1955, ten years after the fact.

There the point is not so much the narrator's grief (real enough) as her realization that her "blameless" life has been worse than not living. I finally wrote my poem about being a nonparticipant, about the guilt of that, and I found after this country had been in Viet Nam for almost ten years that the poem took on new meaning and was again just as valid for me, and valid to be read aloud, as it had seemed originally.

A poem uses everything we know, the surprising things we notice, whatever we can't solve and that keeps on growing, but it has to reach beyond autobiography even to stay on the page. Autobiography is not true enough; it has to be rearranged to release its full meaning. What I see in the poems that now go under the title *Mercator's World* is a rapid wearing-away of assumptions about what a love relationship should and can be between two people. At the time I was writing some of the later poems, these truths seemed terrible. In an early-fifties journal I find the note: "Perhaps I am afraid to write [because] . . . I might kill some comfortable acceptance of myself in the minds of other people, or even in my own mind." (Adrienne Rich has spoken of the need of women writers to be *nice*.) The "you" of the poems is a projection of any one of three men (not who they were but the archetypes I made of them), but also of course there are poems in which the "you" is imaginary, like "Long View from the Suburbs," where, at least partly, I was trying to invent how it might feel to be the old Maud Gonne, whose extraordinary photographs appeared in *Life* magazine. The rhetoric remains heavy (that need to write long lines, to have a battery of sound-effects at my command—like a man?), but, at best, the passion speaks through its frames. In cutting eighty-odd poems down to fifteen, in the end I've wanted to keep only two of the "war" poems: "For a Boy Born in Wartime" and "After the Bomb Tests." In any case, by 1951 the war had begun to seem like a mask, something to write *through* in order to express a desolation that had become personal.

Guilt, war, disease—pillars of violence
To keep a roof of symbols over my head.
Still the rain soaks my bed
Whenever the wind blows, riddling innocence.
A few survive
By the effort of some individual love.

Is this what I thought? that only through an individual
relationship could there be any real survival? By then, or
anyway by a year afterward, with a record of three failed
relationships inside five years, my chances must have seemed
pretty slim.

Why Didn't I Publish?

Why, then, didn't I publish? And why, even more, did I
give up writing poems, and when I went back to poems
eventually change my style, after I'd worked so hard to
make myself into a certain kind of poet during five crucially
formative years? In fact, by the winter of 1951–52, it
felt almost more as if poetry had given me up.

I think it is important to ask these questions just because
I didn't give up poetry for marriage, or to have a baby, or
because the family washing was getting hopelessly ahead of
me. Maybe I gave it up, or put it to one side, precisely
because I still hoped for those things. If this seems cowardly:
"Didn't anyone ever tell you it was all right to write?"
asked the psychiatrist who came along much later. "Yes, but
not to be a writer." Behind me lay the sort of upper-middle-
class education that encourages writing, painting, music,
theater so long as they aren't taken too seriously, so long as
they can be set aside once the real business of life begins.
(But aren't men often blocked in just these same ways?)
I had no women models, as we now understand that word—
and that need. I didn't even know many older women who
worked. Not only my parents but I myself consciously
wanted me to marry and have children. Physical energy was

limited. I write slowly. It was the era which produced *The Feminine Mystique*. And it seems to me even now that the difficulties we all sensed and continue to sense are real and to be respected. I saw clearly how hard it would be for me to make a lasting relationship, bring up children and "live a full life as a woman," while being a committed writer. The women poets I read about were generally not known for their rich, stable sexual and family lives.

Such problems must have faced any young woman of my age who thought of being a poet. Beyond this, each of us can only speak for the problems of her own temperament and her own personal history. As I've already suggested, I was both quite conservative socially at this period and becoming radical in my insights. "Half lover-poet-sybil / Half what the kind nets swallow." An impossible combination. When I first reread the old poems, I was struck by the number that use *seeing* as a metaphor. Seeing equals truth-telling. I wanted to see far, like an astronomer, and I wanted to see through, as if by X rays. But "The urge to tell the truth / Strips sensuality." Domesticity too. If the poems have a virtue that makes some of them worth printing even after all these years, despite their immaturities, despite a blocky, half-borrowed rhetorical style, I think it is not only as a historical record but because of their psychological acuteness. At the same time, a woman painter to whom I showed them not long ago commented on how persistently they seek the "bone," how only the very last ("Obligations," "A Bedside Rune") have any concern for human "breathing." There is a kind of corrosive perfectionism running throughout—a perfectionism that made me end "The Door," in its final draft, with a bid for transcendent union, using an image of X rays for the recognition at zero-level I wanted the lovers to achieve, while another poem about an almost paralyzed affair, "Twins," uses X rays as an image of destructive knowing.

I can't say I didn't recognize how much, if I gave up poetry, I'd be giving up.

49 | *The Manufacture of Poetry*

Foresee me now huddled in my kitchen
Like the woman Ronsard wrote to, shelling peas,
Slag-haired, grained like a rock in the Atlantic,
Having survived the age for lovers and
All subsequent ages, married to the bone
In Greenland. . . .

imagines a marriage which, in its dedication to things of the earth and away from poetry, "will destroy me." "Washing across my face / Look where they drag and scar—the peas, the children." But the truth is, I had come to view poetry as even more destructive. I seemed to have made a mess of my most intimate friendships, and poetry—that gift for seeing far and seeing through—now looked less like a source of renewal (as it had at Oxford) than the house-wrecker. By the winter of 1950–51, though I was still often writing well, I was beginning to be appalled by the images of "guilt, war, disease" that dominated my thinking and kept appearing in the poems almost in spite of myself. Poems like "Meteors" and "After the Bomb Tests" (where Kepler becomes the "virgin artist" and the atomic-bomb explosion mimics human conception and birth) were mirrors into which I couldn't bear to gaze for long.

Teaching

"I see, you had to survive," said one wise friend recently, as she rather quickly laid the old manuscript aside. And indeed, as much as one can by an act of will, I set about to change my life. In September of 1950 I left Princeton to go into teaching, something I had believed in humanly since that summer at Oxford but had kept putting off. I started in at once at Sarah Lawrence, which was certainly more, with only a B.A. and no previous experience, than I deserved. I remember that during one of my interviews I was asked, "And why do you think you can teach poetry?" and I answered, "Because it's the one place where I'd as soon take my own word as anybody else's," though I went on to explain that that didn't mean I thought I was always right! Still, it was eight years before I had a poetry course. I taught fiction, and fiction writing, and to women students. In place of the part-time freelance editing job I was used to, which had left me with free mornings and plenty of free-floating fantasy out of which to write, I was soon working sixty hours a week. I cared very much about those students, and there was everything to learn.

The poems of 1950–51, that first teaching winter, are curiously mixed. I was able to finish several of my angriest early pieces, like "Twins" and "Long View from the Suburbs." I wrote several ambitious new poems ("After the Bomb Tests" started out to be a sonnet-ring) in the old style. At the same time I was beginning to loosen up, to want to use more natural imagery, but also not to be able to develop all I wrote in the old decisive way. This led to its own kind of despair. A poem like "A Bedside Rune" ends so abruptly, the tones of voice are so unbalanced; could you really call it a poem? I didn't yet want poetry to sound like conversation, but the rhetoric I'd been accustomed to and had tried so hard to perfect ("Head first, face down, into Mercator's world") seemed altogether out of keeping with the life I was now leading. I wrote some rather sweet, static new poems about children, landscapes, old men. I don't even remember writing "In a Room with Picassos," where not only the fellow artist but my own role as artist was being put to the test. The most satisfying piece I did all year was "Obligations," which later seemed the last of the old and first of the new, and which was the only poem of the early group to find its way, in somewhat revised form, into my 1969 book. It was the last of the old in that I remember working out the structure quite carefully as a series of abstract geometric figures (the circle that reduces itself to a point, then is opened out again by the "broken shining blade"), which are also of course sexual analogies; meanwhile, however, it is quite an honest poem about an accepted human relationship with its own built-in griefs, and it is set in a stubble field, by daylight, with real insects humming, rather than against some hallucinated sky or sea. One version makes the sexual tie "our defense, which we shall soon evade"; another, the one I have used here because it seems to be the one I eventually settled on, calls it "our defense, which we cannot evade." It was still a time of uncertainty for me, even crisis.

Otto Rank suggested to Anaïs Nin that women have trouble being artists because they damp down what is destructive in them, therefore they can't create freely either. Nin concludes, "In order to create without destroying, I nearly destroyed myself." By the end of 1951, my awareness of crisis had in fact reached a peak. I who had started out asking for equality with the men I knew now wondered whether I had been "castrating." I had a continual, grinding sense of loss and self-betrayal, which only the daily human wear-and-tear of teaching helped somewhat to offset if not change. It was during this second teaching winter that, almost more than my giving up poems, the poems seemed to give me up. What few I wrote were pale and diffuse, or full of self-pity. When I rewrote, I often blurred earlier insights. I was overworked, my health suffered, above all I wanted to learn how to live. By the time I had gone back to writing and, in 1957, was beginning to publish in magazines, I didn't even want to look back at that first manuscript. I remembered it as more destructive than it could ever possibly have been.

Is this primarily a political story, having to do with how hard it is for a woman to *feel* the freedom that would let her develop as a writer, even when she has it? Is it a tale of personal neurosis? Or is it simply the history of one individual woman, probably more twisted than I've allowed here by lovers' claims and family ambitions, in which—as in any history—accident too played a part, but whose echoes may reverberate? For we need all the connections we can make.

En l'an trentiesme de mon aage
Perhaps I shall discover
That each is coward other
And drinking shame, creep into time's cage.

ends the birthday poem I wrote at twenty-three, though it
was an ending I was never really satisfied with. Maybe, I
was saying, instead of feeling "wiser" and more secure by
the time I reached thirty, I'd find out instead that to be
either "lover-poet-sybil" *or* a housewife would be a kind of
cowardice, because I couldn't be both? Since each would be
only a half-life, maybe they would add up to the same
life? The final "cage" might not be a matter of choice at
all but the necessary compromises of aging, of facing myself.
Even then I had the foretaste of shame, like a numbing drug.

A Room of My Own, with Windows

I have said that I gave up poetry, but after all it seems
as if I never quite gave up the idea of writing. To have been
convinced for so long that I gave it up altogether may
have been the last deception I practiced on myself in con-
nection with that early work, those early years. For I still
have the journal I kept during the winter and spring of
1952–53, the year before I went to Iowa to (as I told every-
body) observe teaching methods at the Writers' Workshop
there. I hadn't been at Iowa more than three or four weeks
before I was deep in stories of my own and, once more,
poems. By the second semester the stories had been laid
aside. . . . But what the journal documents is that it was
started deliberately as a way of getting me back to writing,
through the sanity of observed detail, and that I had begun
to think seriously about fiction. Fiction might prove a more
humane mode than poetry. Did I also have some idea (the
journal doesn't say so) that to be a woman short-story writer
might be more acceptable than being a poet?

Most of all I wanted to get people into what I wrote—

people who were not mere projections of my own needs and angers but people walking around and talking, recognizably *other*, as unique and often funny as my students had turned out to be. If seeing was the metaphor for truth-telling in the poems that lay just behind me, seeing from the height of an airplane or with the intensity of X rays, then looking was what I aimed for by 1953, truly looking at the world around me and trying to record it. I was touched by Ransom's notion that it is the specific detail, intimately rendered, that reveals our love for a subject. Much of the journal is simply notes I took out my New York City windows. In the fall of 1952 I had moved to a walk-up on West Sixteenth Street, between Seventh and Eighth Avenues, and this neighborhood was shocking me awake in a new way. In my mind was that room I always remember, again from the summer of 1947, in heavily shelled St. Mâlo: *Two walls of an old stone building are still standing, up one of which a stone staircase climbs crazily toward nothing. Halfway up, pitched over space and rubble, is cantilevered a brand-new timber box— yellow, fresh-smelling, inhabited—with a potted red geranium in its one immaculate window-square.*

For despite my memory of the strain of those years, the journal is honest, strong, feeling, and it even has a kind of natural gaiety. It speaks of the necessity for changing myself, for finding a new style both of being and writing, to go with the changed realities I now perceived. It explores what might be required for short stories and outlines a good many plots. Because the mechanistic imagery I had used so far had begun to horrify me, and certainly contradicted in human intent and almost in coloration what I wanted to do next, it suggests that a new imagery must be found, less like a crustacean's shell. But to change one's images is like trying to revolutionize one's dreams. It can't be done overnight. Nor can it be effected by will. I find one entry reading: "Something seems to have broken in me last year, like a spring breaking. . . . What broke . . . is perhaps the sense that you can build your life by choice. Now I think you build it out of necessities—and that all you can do is answer these necessities in the decentest way possible. . . . I am trying to learn to lead a decent life and not want to be a great person and, at the same time, know what I have the human right to draw the line at."

"Not want to be a great person." ("To be a man, the crowd's hero.") I was jolted when I discovered those words written out, for how rarely we admit we want to be great persons. Women's need to appear modest, certainly my own need, is almost as powerful as the need to be nice, and no doubt not at all separate from it.

The journal gives specific reasons for the failure of the poems of the previous five years and even of my whole conception of poetry. Too "musical," for one thing. "I think first of all in terms of a very definite rhythm and structure. Emotionally, too, I think in terms of rhetoric, of an impassioned dramatization of a moment. . . . Now I can no longer capture those moods . . . and so the whole rhetorical machinery seems . . . out of date. My poetry was heroic poetry, and now what I have to say doesn't concern heroes, and I haven't the heart to change the machinery, taking out a screw here and a blade there, to make it something different, and less, than it was. . . . The poetry I have written this year is just empty mechanics or else it hardly comes into being."

Again: "I have a very old-fashioned idea of what poetry should do. It is the soul's history and whatever troubles the soul is fit material for poetry. Therefore I was right to try to write war poems, even if they were often overblown, because no one can live just personally, just observing the workings of his own consciousness, these days. Now I am trying to write [about] love—but giving the quality of the other person."

And finally: "To begin with, love is a joyful recognition of capacities within yourself. It is yourself you fall in love with. Much later, perhaps, the individual with whom you are in love comes to mean more than the condition of 'being in love.' For some people this means a comedown to what they call friendship; for others, it is marriage. . . . The first abstract stage is the stage of poetry. Does the second stage imply fiction, or just a different kind of poetry, a poetry of development rather than passionate lyrical statement?"

How much one would like to be able to argue with one's younger self! And yet was this conception of poetry—that it should be heroic, "musical" (*i.e.*, romantically metrical, with "a very definite rhythm and structure"), and even abstract—so different from that other conception, which I'd been brought up to and wanted to believe, that I should find the *solution* to my life, not just companionship, in a single, other person? (And that I still wanted marriage, the imagery of the last paragraph makes perfectly clear.) The final version of "The Door" showed what a weight this put on the men I knew, as well as on myself. They had to be heroic, and not the least of my mistakes lay in blaming myself when it turned out, humanly enough, to be otherwise.

But most of the journal is not so didactic, nor even particularly meditative. I was living on a half-Irish, half-Puerto Rican block, and I wrote about the boys burning Christmas greens in the gutters in January; about the soft-drink bar where the older boys hung out, smoking, perched on orange crates along the sidewalk, almost under the lee of a crumbling brownstone called "Rainbow"; I recorded the little girls' street games and some of their chants. When one day in May an amusement truck came along, shaped like a gigantic popcorn popper with loudspeakers on top—and as the children were jounced down and then up inside almost to the height of the first-story windows one cried "Hey look at the sky!"—I made a rough sketch of the truck body with approximate dimensions. I thought of the windows across the street from mine as eye-pairs, two to a family, into which I could look and which would sometimes stare back at me out of their separate, never-fully-to-be-understood worlds.

An Art of the Unexpected

My getting back to poems again, the following year, is really another story. I think I am still trying to work out a "poetry of development." And certainly when I first started at Iowa I had to face the embarrassment (to call it by a mild name) of knowing that what I wrote was far weaker, from any standpoint but my own, than what I had been doing three or four years before. It was after all not just a matter of "taking out a screw here and a blade there, to make . . . something different." My whole intention as a writer had changed. In trying for a more generous habit of mind, for instance, whether deliberately or not I set aside the kind of anger that often goes along with sexuality as one of the pivots of my work. I wonder how many women share with me this history, of not having wanted to admit their anger? I did write as an observer, almost too patiently. For a while children, landscapes, old men predominated. It is very difficult to practice any art wholeheartedly and not to compromise, at least now and then, teaching as well as maternal roles, community responsibility. There is the problem of self-centeredness, if not outright selfishness. On the other hand, for writers especially, just because they use words, it is hard to be generous and never to indulge in self-censorship.

These questions that confront women writers (and of course, many men too) are, far more than the questions I opened with, the ones that continue to trouble me. How are we to balance our needs? It's unlikely that any young woman poet today would simply suppress her work, as I did. And I wish I hadn't. Yet I can't be sorry that *The Weather of Six Mornings*, when it finally appeared, was based on certain rather broad human acceptances. I had to get through the perfectionism of those early poems, to learn that no choice is absolute and no structure can save us. If I no longer hesitate to bring out a few pages from that first manuscript, the questions are just as urgent as they ever were. All the more reason, I think, to accept as part of whatever I now am that young, cabined, often arrogant, but questing and vivid self whose banishment I've come to recognize as one more mistaken absolute. For if my poems have always been about survival—and I believe they have been—then survival too keeps revealing itself as an art of the unexpected.

New York, 1974

III

Mercator's World

Poems 1947–1951

Mercator, 1512–94. Flemish geographer, mathematician, and
cartographer. . . . In 1568 appeared his first map using the
projection which has since borne his name and which has been
more generally used than any other projection for navigators'
maps of the world.

Mercator's projection is of great value to navigators, since it
shows true directions, but it has great disadvantages for general
use. The parallels and meridians are represented as straight lines,
intersecting at right angles. The length of a degree of latitude
is thus represented as the same in higher latitudes as it is at the
equator. To preserve the correct proportion between a degree
of longitude and a degree of latitude, the length of a degree
of longitude must be correspondingly increased, and the result
is a misrepresentation of areas and distances, increasing with
distance from the equator. In a MAP on Mercator's projection,
Greenland appears larger than South America, and Alaska
comparable in size with the United States. . . . Of course, also,
it is impossible to represent at all the areas very near the poles.

—*The Columbia Encyclopedia*, 1945

Eve

Now she is still not beautiful but more
Moving than before, for time has come
When she shall be delivered; some-
one must have, move her, or the doors
Be shuttered over, the doorlids shut, her
Eyes' lies shattered. In the spume
Of a triple wave she lives: sperm,
Man and life's mate break like flags upon her shore.

Marriage must take her now, or the sly
Inquirer, inviting her to ship for his sake,
Will share all islands inland with her, her sky
No one else shares, will slake
Conquerlust. Seas wash away her ties
While through her thigh-trees water strikes like a snake.

1947

For a Boy Born in Wartime

Head first, face down, into Mercator's world
Like an ungainly rocket the child comes
Driving dead-reckoned outward through a channel
Where nine months back breath was determined
By love, leaving his watery pen—
That concrete womb with its round concrete walls
Which he could make a globe of all his own—
For flatter dryer enemies, for home.

Boy we have set in motion like an engine,
Bound by our instruments no one knows where
Until upending you are zero London,
Headlong from water, what will you make of air?
An empire? light to whistle through? a ball
To bounce? Or will your tumbling feet
Drop down and inward to the concrete
Unmalleable mirror world we live in,

Inheritor of our geographies,
Just as we rise to slap your fluttering cry?

1949

a poem with capital letters

john berryman asked me to write a poem about roosters.
elizabeth bishop, he said, once wrote a poem about roosters.
do your poems use capital letters? he asked. like god?
i said. *god no*, he said, *like princeton!* i said,
god preserve me if i ever write a poem about princeton! and
    i thought,
o john berryman, what has brought me into this company of
    poets
where the masculine thing to do is use capital letters
and even princeton's cock-a-hoop with god's betters?

1948

The Door

Intelligent companion,
Talented—yes, and blind—but can
I live the pitiful part I play?
For what do you see when I
Come to you? Isn't it woman,
Passion, a pair of eyes, the ground
To prove old sex and sorrows on?
Tomorrow, if you were blinded
Really, physically, could you
Picture me as I come through
This door? Could you construct a me,
All physical reality,
And then, easy as light,
Penetrate the lips I speak from,
Plant them with speech or start
Thought with your kisses?
                                        I am
A person after all. You are
A person. We are proud and fear
The same things: pride of possession,
Cowardice, communication
Stopped.
              Silhouetted in this door
I stop a moment like a stranger
Before the darkness. What do you see?
I wait for tongues, then eyes to join,
Intelligent, companions.

1948

The Urge To Tell the Truth

The urge to tell the truth
Strips sensuality
Like bark stripped from a tree.
Bone-nakedness and growth
Are incompatible;
The stripped tree falls.

After the squirrels finish,
The white squirrels of the brain,
Such naturalness is driven
From the body's wish,
Such diffidence and humor,
That a white score

Of toothmarks at the root
Of unity is all
The tree surgeon reveals,
Past mending with concrete;
And sycamore and oak
And marriage break.

1949

Christmas Letter

December is our month, a long season
And only at the end of it this birth,
Annihilating—like an uncertain treason—
Flake by flake what I know of earth

And you of miracle. Creators,
We stand about like cattle in the cold,
Weary of guilt, watching the sun go under.
Of all months, this one is old.

Yet at the end, which is distrust, which vision?
Something is born and flickers on the night:
A child perhaps or a late poem
Or something shared, though it is very late.

1949–51

Twins

You ask for love but what you want is healing,
Selfishly, understandably. You pray
For marriage as another man might pray
For sleep after surgery, failing
More ether, miraculous cure by a saint
Or the tissues still uncut. You want
Never again to look at incompleteness,
Yours or mine or ours; this is our weakness.

All the images you use are of darkness—
Sleep, forgiveness, physical unity
Transcending daylight bodies and the rays
Where a Curie works or wounded priests confess—
You won't believe you're maimed, you won't believe
There is any other way to live
Than whole. You're as careful of your honor
As any cripple; this is our humor.

But I'm ashamed—shamed by the doctors
You've prayed to in the hope someone might close
Your eyes in passion, shamed that I expose
And kill and heal you with the simplest finger.
I'm radium, apocalypse in the breast;
I understand—this is my selfishness.
And while love dies cancered by light, I
Hesitate and can neither live nor die.

1949–51

The Knowledge That Comes Through Experience

I feel my face being bitten by the tides
Of knowledge as sea-tides bite at a beach;
Love leaves its implications, wars encroach
On the flat white square between my ear and jaw
Picking it as the sea hollows out sand. . . .
I might as well stick my head in the maw

Of the ocean as live this generously:
Feelings aside I never know my face;
I comb my hair and what I see is timeless,
Not a face at all but (besides the hair)
Lips and a pair of eyes, two hands, a body
Pale as a fish imprisoned in the mirror.

When shall I rest, when shall I find myself
The way I'll be, iced in a shop window?
Maybe I'll wake tonight in the undertow
Of sleep and lie adrift, gutted helpless
By the salt at my blue eyes—then the gulfs
Of looks and desire will shine clean at last.

Meanwhile I use myself. I am useful
Rather foolishly, like a fish who yearns
Dimly toward daylight. There is much to learn
And curiosity riddles our rewards.
It seems to me I may be capable
Once I'm a skeleton, of love and wars.

1950

Long View from the Suburbs

Yes I'm the lady he wrote the sonnets to.
I can tell you how it was
And where the books lie, biographies and his
Famous later versions now collected
In one volume for lovers. (You
Can never really analyze his method

If you only read those.) Once for instance
He begged to meet me under an oak
Outside the city after five o'clock.
It was early April. I waited there
Until in the distance
A streetlight whitened on the sensual air.

Then I walked home again. The next day
He was touchy and elated
Because of a new poem which he said
Marked some advance—perhaps that "honest" style
Which prostitutes our memories—
He gave it to me. I said nothing at all

Being weary. It had happened so often.
He was always deluding himself,
Complaining (honestly) that I spurned his gifts.
Shall I tell you what gifts are? Although I said
Nothing at the time
I still remember evenings when I learned

The tricks of style. Do you know, young man,
Do they teach you in biographies

How it feels to open like a city
At the caress of darkness, then sickening
To walk about alone
Until a streetlamp yawns in reckoning?

1949–51

In a Room with Picassos

Draw as you will there are no images
Which exactly reproduce this state of mind!
No bull can satisfy my unspoken anger
Or Spanish boys speak plainly for my love
While you refuse it. I can stand and stand
In front of canvas and artistic paraphernalia
But nothing there will answer me with pride:
I am the exact shade of shame and desire,
Your justification in the face of his
Simple indifference to simple fire.
I am the offering which always moves
Anyone, no matter how far away he is from love.

1950–51

After the Bomb Tests

1

The atom bellies like a cauliflower,
Expands, expands, shoots up again, expands
Into ecclesiastical curves and towers
We pray to with our cupped and empty hands.
This is the old Hebraic-featured fear
We nursed before humility began,
Our crown-on-crown, our phallic parody
Begot by man on the original sea.

The sea's delivered. Galvanized and smooth
She kills a tired ship left in her lap
—Transfiguration—with a half-breath
Settling like an animal in sleep.
So godhead takes the difficult forms of love.
Where is the little myth we used to have?

2

Where is the simple myth we used to have?
The childish mother and her fatherless son,
That infinitesimal act, creation,
Which shocks two cells so that they melt and solve
A riddle of light and all our darkness tears
With meanings like struck water round a stone?
Is it all gone? Are the meanings gone?

I walk out of the house into the still air,
Moving from circle to circle—hot, cold,
Like zones of water this October night.
All the stars are still arranged in spheres,
The planets stalk serenely. Thinking of Kepler
I pick a grassblade, chew it up, then spit.
Now I have thought, he cried, *the thoughts of God!*

3

Now I have thought the very thoughts of God!
Mentally checking the sky he doused his lamp
And let the worlds come to life within him.
And if he were wrong? Could one harmony hold
The sum of private freedoms like a cup?
He gazed outward. Affectionately, delicately,
Distance received him in a lap of sleep;
He felt its warm muzzle on his eye.
He smiled, darkening. He had caged the sky.

When he woke up dawn stretched like a canvas,
Empty and deep. Over the slick seal river
A wind skated. Kepler, curious, rose,
Started to cross himself—then like a lover
Or virgin artist gave himself to his power.

1950–51

Gaza

Too calm to beg for pity yet too strained
Ever to call my bluff or disown me
Openly, you said nothing but remained
Masterful—I thought weak—solitary,
Like one of those old kings without a face
Who grip in tiers of weatherbeaten stone
The O of a cathedral carapace:
Unmouthed, you groped like Samson to be dethroned.

1950–51

Meteors

Whom can we love in all these little wars?
The aviator, king of his maps and glowing lights
But dispossessed of six-foot-two of ground?
The sailor, blind as a worm, suspended
In a hammock made of scrap iron, in his fear
Heavy and liquid to the touch as night?

Whom can we love? The same question
Asked five years back drops through my ear and dies
With a fizzle of brightness at the center of my brain.
The sky is streaked with pilots falling. I see
Buried in altitude like meteors
Cartoons of wit and sex, skeletons of leaders.

1950–51

A Bedside Rune

Not jealousy but pale disgust complains:
So here's what all those gentle manners come to!
Meaning ourselves, meaning the three years' passion
We've watched over like a sick child

All day and night. Only last night I sat
Waiting for a heartbeat like an old woman
Rocking away: *Life-death* her rockers say,
Death-life sighed the small heartbeat.

1950–51

Obligations

Here where we are, wrapped in the afternoon
As in a chrysalis of silken light,
Our bodies kindly holding one another
Against the press of vision from outside,
Here where we clasp in a stubble field
Is all the safety either of us hopes for,
Stubbornly constructing walls of night
Out of the ordered energies of the sun.

With the same gratitude I feel the hot
Dazzle on my eyelids and your hand
Carefully opening my shaded breasts.
The air is very high and still. The buzz
And tickle of an insect glow and fuse
Into the flicker of a pulse. We rest
Closed in the golden shallows of a sound
Till, opening my eyes, I accept your trust.

My fingers pick at a broken shining blade
Of stubble as you bend to look at me.
What can I do to help you? Some extreme
Unction of the act of love is on us.
The act itself has built this sphere of anguish
Which we must now inhabit like our dreams,
The dark home of our polarities
And our defense, which we cannot evade.

1950–51

Notes

I

Feathers: First line is from one of Zhivago's poems in Pasternak's *Doctor Zhivago*, translation by Bernard Guilbert Guerney.

El Sueño de la Razón: A nightmare etching by Goya is inscribed *El sueño de la razón produce monstruos: The dream of reason begets monsters.*

Our Lady of Light: One of a series of poems by the contemporary Brazilian, João Cabral de Melo Neto, all under the general title *Cemetery in Pernambuco.* Pernambuco is a state in northeastern Brazil, and Cabral's concern is for the peasants, mostly sugarcane-cutters, there.

Inheritances: Taken almost verbatim from M. D. Herter Norton's translation of Rilke's *The Notebooks of Malte Laurids Brigge.*

II

page 31: See Tillie Olsen's "Silences When Writers Don't Write," *Harper's Magazine*, October, 1965. Among other things Olsen lists the important women writers of the nineteenth century who never married and points to the surprisingly large number even in this century who have remained single or, at any rate, childless.

page 31: Dream Song 187 from Berryman's *His Toy, His Dream, His Rest.*

page 52: *Diary of Anaïs Nin*, 1934–39, p. 31: "Rank believes that to create it is necessary to destroy. Woman cannot destroy. He believes that may be why she has rarely been a great artist. In order to create without destroying, I nearly destroyed myself."

III

After the Bomb Tests: I was thinking of the United States tests at Bikini Atoll in the Marshall Islands, Western Pacific, in 1946. Kepler (1571–1630) formulated the laws of planetary motion.